The challenge of photographing the TT

SHUTTER SPEED

Dave Collister and Mick Duckworth

Published by Lily Publications Ltd, PO Box 33, Ramsey, Isle of Man, British Isles, IM99 4LP

Tel: +44 (0) 1624 898446   Fax: +44 (0) 1624 898449

www.lilypublications.co.uk

FOREWORD

By John McGuinness, winner of 15 TT races and holder of the outright Mountain Course lap record at 131.578mph.

As a successful TT rider, you get to know all the regular photographers by sight. But there are only a few whose face and name you can match to particular shots you have seen in print. Dave Collister is one of them.

When I first got talking to Dave a few years ago during a magazine shoot on the Isle of Man, I realised that he took some of my all-time favourite Mountain Course action photos.

Just as I set out to learn every inch of the TT Course, Dave scours its 37.73 miles for good spots to take photos from. He sets himself high standards and I know his research is thorough, because he comes up to me in the paddock and asks if my bike wheelies here or gets airborne there. If I'm feeling in a generous mood I tell him!

I am pleased to introduce this truly mega collection of Dave's TT photos, which capture the spectacular action and unique atmosphere of Mountain Course racing, set in the Isle of Man's beautiful scenery. A book for all road racing fans to enjoy and treasure, it will also show anyone who has never been to the TT just what they are missing.

Two legends. Top TT ace McGuinness with Moto GP maestro Valentino Rossi at the 2009 TT.

Total control. A Dave Collister shot of McGuinness on a 1000cc Honda FireBlade at the famous Ago's Leap that follows the Bray Hill descent.

FOCUS ON THE TT

A start line shot from 1985. As a child Dave Collister watched from only a few yards away.

Chief timekeeper John Stott flags riders away at 10-second intervals in 1999.

The Isle of Man Tourist Trophy motorcycle races have an incomparable place in the world of motor sport. They are held on the formidable Mountain Course, a 37.73mile circuit formed from roads normally in use as public highways. Temporary road closures for racing are made possible by legislation first passed by the Island's semi-autonomous government in 1904. Since the demise of the Targa Florio and Mille Miglia car racing epics in the Fifties, the TT stands alone as the last of the long-circuit road races.

A peculiarity of Mountain Course racing is that competitors start at strictly timed intervals, so they race against the clock rather than directly against each other, although thrilling wheel-to-wheel dices between evenly matched riders are not unknown.

No other high-speed motorcycle event makes such demands of both machine and rider as the TT. The Course passes through suburbs and villages, winds through a river gorge and unfurls across high moorland reaching a maximum altitude just short of 430m (1,400ft) on its mountain section, following a climb from near sea level. There are long, relatively straight stretches where the most powerful bikes are nudging 200mph and severe hairpin bends where they must slow to near walking pace. In places the road is as smooth as a motorway, while some sections have ripples and bumps that challenge the most sophisticated suspension systems and destruction-test the sturdiest chassis components.

Unlike a purpose-built race-track, the roads used as the TT Course are bordered by immovable objects like kerbs, gateposts, telephone poles, steel railings, stone walls and bus shelters. Strenuous efforts are made to minimise their potentially lethal danger with air bags and soft bales, but it is impossible to cushion every solid roadside object. And no-one has total control over seagulls or other wildlife. Every competitor is aware that a minor error can result in the ultimate penalty. Obviously an exceptional level of concentration is called for and any rider hoping for success needs to acquire an intimate knowledge of the 220-odd corners, learning the best lines and how to flow them together to achieve the optimum average speed over the 37-plus miles. The lap record currently stands at more than 131mph for solo motorcycles and 116mph for sidecar outfits.

Such a long lap cannot be learned quickly and each TT Week, usually running from Saturday to the following Friday, is preceded by a week long practice period. Until 2004, the roads were closed for early morning training sessions and until 2007 there was a traditional Thursday afternoon session, when conditions were nearest to those likely for racing. While a typical meeting for bike racers is a long weekend, the TT is a two-week commitment at least.

Today's top TT riders tend to be 'real roads' specialists, who excel on the Isle of Man and other public road courses like those in Ireland, rather than in the cut-and-thrust of racing on artificial circuits. There are exceptions, notably 2009 Senior TT winner Steve Plater who also took the championship in the hectic British Supersport series in the same year.

The challenges and undoubted perils of TT racing foster a strong camaraderie between competitors. Instances of intentionally dangerous

Nick Jefferies (Castrol Honda) passes
a bus shelter grandstand at Ballaugh in
1995.

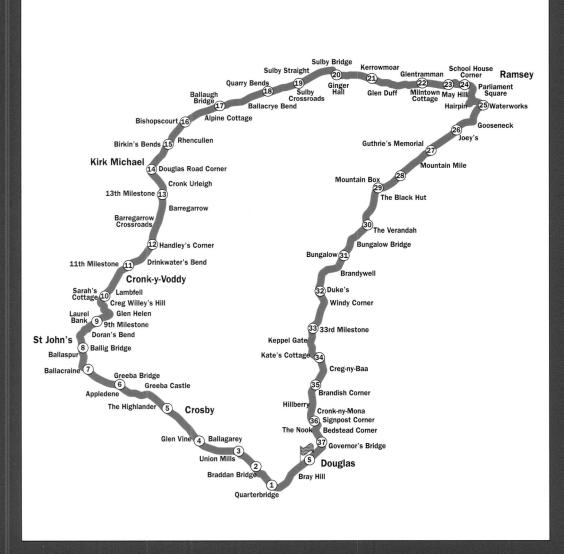

The map shows the Mountain Course circuit with numbered locations:

- Sulby Bridge
- Sulby Straight
- Kerrowmoar
- Glentramman
- School House Corner
- Ramsey
- Quarry Bends (18)
- Sulby Crossroads (19)
- Ginger Hall (20)
- (21)
- Glen Duff
- (22) Milntown Cottage (23) (24) May Hill
- Parliament Square
- Ballaugh Bridge (17)
- Ballacrye Bend
- (25) Waterworks
- Alpine Cottage
- Hairpin
- Bishopscourt (16)
- Gooseneck
- (26) Joey's
- Birkin's Bends (15) Rhencullen
- Guthrie's Memorial
- (27)
- Kirk Michael
- Mountain Mile
- (14) Douglas Road Corner
- Mountain Box
- (28)
- Cronk Urleigh
- (29)
- 13th Milestone (13)
- The Black Hut
- Barregarrow
- (30) The Verandah
- Barregarrow Crossroads
- Bungalow Bridge
- (12) Handley's Corner
- Bungalow (31)
- 11th Milestone (11) Drinkwater's Bend
- Brandywell
- Cronk-y-Voddy
- (32) Duke's
- Sarah's Cottage (10) Lambfell
- Windy Corner
- Creg Willey's Hill
- Laurel Bank
- (33) 33rd Milestone
- (9) 9th Milestone
- Glen Helen
- Keppel Gate
- Doran's Bend
- St John's
- Kate's Cottage (34)
- (8) Ballig Bridge
- Creg-ny-Baa
- Ballaspur
- (35)
- Ballacraine (7)
- Brandish Corner
- Greeba Bridge
- Hillberry
- Cronk-ny-Mona
- (6) Greeba Castle
- (36) Signpost Corner
- Appledene
- The Nook
- Bedstead Corner
- The Highlander (5) Crosby
- (37) Governor's Bridge
- Glen Vine (4) Ballagarey
- (3)
- Union Mills
- (S) Douglas
- (2)
- Braddan Bridge
- Bray Hill
- (1)
- Quarterbridge

The 37.73 miles of the Mountain Course offer almost limitless possibilities to photographers.

Cornering on air. Darran Lindsay flies
through Union Mills in 2005.

riding are rare, as is arrogant and boastful behaviour.

Riders who perform well but don't reach the winners' podium receive replicas of the magnificent TT winner's trophy. Finishing within 105 per cent of the winner's race time earns a Silver Replica and coming within 110 per cent merits a Bronze Replica. All other finishers receive a medal.

From the onlooker's point of view, the TT offers an unparalleled and sometimes heart-stopping spectacle. Many of the best vantage points can be accessed without charge and even after recent moves to minimise the risk of injury, or worse, to spectators there are places where you can much closer to the action than is possible at a typical racing circuit. Some viewing spots are only accessible while the

roads are open, while others are easy to reach at any time. It is possible to watch the racing from bedroom windows, front gardens or from one of the several pubs adjacent to the Course.

As they are gunned around the Mountain Course the bikes bounce off bumps, stand on their back wheels, squirm under heavy braking and sometimes shimmy alarmingly. Speeds have increased to a point where much of the visual drama happens so quickly it can barely be caught by the human eye. As a result, both video and less transient still photography have increased in importance to the TT fan.

Amateur and professional photographers converge on the TT from all over the world seeking images that capture the excitement and atmosphere. But only a few get really crisp and dynamic results. Like TT riding, Mountain Course photography is an art within an art, with its own particular challenges and rewards. As well as mastering the technicalities of making images, a good TT photographer needs to be hardy, patient and resourceful.

Isle of Man-based Dave Collister, whose superb photography fills this book, is undoubtedly one of its best current practitioners. So, over to him to tell us about himself and show us a selection of his best and most evocative images from the last three decades.

Two of the very best: David Jefferies and John McGuinness on the Devonshire Road jump in 2002 practice.

It's easy to explain where my love of motorcycle racing comes from. The house where I grew up was just a short walk away from the TT start and finish area on Glencrutchery Road. We lived on the inside of the Course and by the time I was ten I had my own favourite spot, in a tree that virtually overlooked the start line. From there I had a fantastic view of the race, probably better than from the Grandstand across the road. And it was free!

I had a very basic camera from an early age, but in my teens I got my first proper equipment, a second-hand 35mm Minolta SLR with a 70-200mm zoom lens. When my long-suffering parents also bought me a black and white developing kit, the back washhouse became my makeshift darkroom. I loved that side of photography because it gave control over the whole process from pressing the shutter to watching a picture magically appear in the gently rocking developing dish.

Naturally, I was drawn to photographing the TT but was always interested in finding my own places rather than going to all the obvious ones.

Back in the Seventies and Eighties the two TT photographers I really rated while leafing through *Motorcycle Racing* or *Motor Cycle Weekly* were Don Morley and Nick Nicholls. They were the benchmarks, the governors, whose shots captured the essence of what the TT was about and were more than just photos of motorcycles on a road.

In 1982 I had a part-time job cleaning motorcycles in a Douglas shop and one day the mechanics were talking about this hallowed place called Ballacrye, a jump about three-quarters of a mile beyond Ballaugh Bridge. I had never heard of

the place - few people had in those days - but they said I should look for a house with a cross on the gable and not tell anyone else but keep it as a secret among locals.

For Thursday's afternoon practice I cycled the 17-odd miles to Ballaugh, and found the house (there is an X-shaped iron brace on the end wall) but couldn't see a jump. Sceptical that I was the victim of a windup but with the road about to close, I found somewhere safe to stand in a field on the inside of the Course. When the first bikes came through I was just staggered, there was enough of a crest on the road to make their front wheels stand right up, with fast riders like Joey Dunlop and Mick Grant going

VIEW FROM THE HEDGES

Ready for action. Dave Collister in roadside shooting mode. (Lily Publications)

Dave Collister sets off in a 250cc Manx GP race, 1992. (David Purves)

and soil is softer than tarmac. I fell off a lot and missed riding on the road. With the 1988 TT fast approaching, a used Yamaha TZR250 Sarron Replica appeared in a local bike shop. It was too much to resist and so the trusty - and a bit rusty - XR was sold.

The TZR went and handled so well that I tore round the TT Course like a complete juvenile practically every fine evening. I even timed my work journey from Douglas to Castletown: stupid stuff, but speed is an addictive drug.

I got my comeuppance in 1989 when I was clocked at over 100mph in a 30mph limit. In my defence, I was braking hard going past the 30 sign. No, that didn't wash with the judge either, and I got a three-month ban.

The TZR was sold, the proceeds going towards yet more camera gear, and with too much kit to carry on a bike, a car became my preferred transport.

Because of increased traffic on the roads, a lot of my mates were giving up road bikes to go racing. It is the only way to find out how fast you really are and I'd always fancied doing the Manx Grand Prix club races on the Mountain Course, although it would take at least two years to get the required National Licence. Throwing caution to the wind, I bought a Yamaha TZ350 but it turned out be a totally unreliable money pit. After the acute embarrassment of high-siding in front of a packed grandstand at Carnaby Raceway on the last lap when in last place, I sold the mangled bike and packed up.

After a couple of years, the itch to go racing was too much and I bought another TZ, this time a 1987

completely airborne, at such a speed that I didn't get a single decent shot. The pace was so much faster than I was used to and my lens too short.

In 1984 I signed on as an accredited pass holder for the first time, and having turned 17 I had my first bike, a Suzuki GSX250. That was handy for getting around with my growing bag of camera equipment but within a year I was skittled off by a car that pulled out in front of me in Douglas. I was knocked out and had a fractured pelvis, but blew the insurance payout on a Honda XR250 dirt bike and even more camera equipment.

The idea was that riding off-road would be safer

250cc T series. Three of my mates, Kev, Rob and Mugsy chipped in to help and we called ourselves Well Hard Racing. In reality, it was more like Hard Up Racing as we couldn't really afford the running costs.

We had the best laugh immersing ourselves in the local racing scene, going to all the meetings at the Jurby circuit in 1991 to build up to the required 20 signatures for that elusive National Licence. Money was so tight we didn't even have our own van, but someone lent us one on condition we taxed and insured it. Trouble was that the owner used it for clearing household junk in the week and didn't always get round to emptying the van before we had it at weekends.

I gained my National Licence just in time to enter the 1992 Southern 100 on the Billown Circuit. In the 250cc race, a rider contesting the lead went up the inside of me at Ballanorris. Finding it a little too close for comfort, instead of taking the corner I shot straight through Joey's Gate, a farm gate left open during races as a slip route. It was named after the great Joey Dunlop who went through it in 1979.

I ended up sliding off in the field right through piles of cow dung and my indignity was compounded when I was refused the normal lift back to the paddock in the course car. With the window wound down an inch I was told by the Clerk of the Course: "You're not getting in here stinking of shit!"

In that year's Manx GP I was helped by local racing buff Roger Owen and got my 100mph lap by Tuesday of practice week, so achieved my main target. Bike trouble stopped me in the Lightweight Newcomers race and I finished 14th in the very wet Lightweight, narrowly missing a Silver Replica by four seconds.

Full credit to Roger for coming up with an oversize fuel tank that let me do three laps with only one stop. Credit also has to go to my pit crew of Kev and Mugsy for bungling my pitstop, earning them an expletive-strewn rollicking that took a lot longer than the critical four seconds. What I didn't know was that Manx Radio commentator Geoff Cannell was right behind me with his roving microphone. The full barrage of expletives was broadcast live, as I later learned to my embarrassment in my local pub.

Only inches from the road, spectators in Ramsey gasp at a near-miss during a 1998 Sidecar race.

Michael Dunlop celebrates a moving 2009 Supersport victory.

Looking back, all of the above sums up my racing career: a comedy of errors and near-misses but a good time was had by all. Realising that I could afford either racing or serious photography but not both, I opted to stick with cameras.

Meanwhile, I'd had my first black and white photos published in a spread on the 1985 Manx GP in Road Racing Monthly. I started dabbling in colour and made the changeover to the splendours of Kodachrome transparency film in 1988. While it was the ultimate in quality, the snag was you had to send it to Paris to be processed and waiting days or even weeks to see the results could be nerve-wracking. But nothing compares to the anticipation of tearing the packet open to squint through a magnifying loupe at a perfectly exposed, pin-sharp slide on the lightbox.

Eventually I was forced to make the switch to digital photography in 2003. By then digital SLR cameras had progressed enough technically to be acceptable for magazine work, where speed as well as high definition is vital. But, like many other photographers, I still believe that the best transparency film is hard to beat for its quality of colour and saturation.

Never one for following the pack, I always try to find a deserted spot to get away from other photographers. For me, the crush around the winner's rostrum following a race with 50 cameras all taking the same shot isn't what TT photography is about. Editors do need those shots but I won't sacrifice remote but outstanding locations just to rush back and cover every winners' podium.

Having said that, I regret missing the podium ceremony after Joey Dunlop's amazing Formula 1 win in 2000 and I felt that his nephew Michael's emotional first TT win in last year's Supersport was a must.

Living on the Isle of Man gives me the advantage that I can drive round the Course all year round to recce for new angles. I get ideas from watching TV footage of the racing, which is really amazing these days, and talking to riders to find out where they are getting airborne or out of shape, as the bikes get faster and small alterations are made to the road surfaces, these things can change a photograph year on year.

A good example is the Union Mills bridge, a much-photographed spot now, where back in the winter of 2001 I noticed the road had subsided, exaggerating the camber. I guessed it might turn the usual front wheel hop into something more spectacular. It certainly did and my shot of TT legend Ian Lougher fully airborne while cranked over in the 2002 Senior race was published across two pages.

Knowing my way around the back roads is essential for shooting a race from more than one section. One of the particular demands of TT racing is that with such a long lap, riders only go past you a maximum of six times in any race, that is a lot different from a short circuit where they might come by every couple of minutes for anything up to 30 times in a main race.

Predicting light conditions can be a problem, but the TT's week of practising gives you a chance to 'bank' some shots and take a few risks with a full week of racing to follow. Also the quality of light

during a late evening Practice can be better: in some cases the press prefer those shots to race day pics.

Not being a staff or agency photographer gives me more freedom and while I have considered becoming a full-time professional bike photographer the only real chance I had came and went. Luckily, when TT time comes round, I have a sympathetic employer.

There is another thing that sets the TT apart from circuits like Donington Park or Silverstone, where only someone with a pass can hope to get the best shots. The Mountain Course offers almost endless scope and opportunity for anyone with enough luck or imagination to pull off a once-in-a lifetime shot.

Even with a photographer's pass, you can't just go where you please and in recent years several places have been made prohibited areas in the interests of safety. It can be frustrating, but it is understandable and I must admit that there are locations I've used that were so dangerous I would never go back.

It's basic good manners to get permission to go in people's front gardens or other obviously private areas and I've rarely had problems. The days when marshals let you run along the pavement when the road was quiet have gone, so sometimes it's a matter of clambering through bushes and ducking under barbed wire. My worst terror is crossing fields where there are cattle, especially young calves. They follow you out of curiosity and if you speed up, so do they. There are times when it must look like the Running of the Bulls in Pamplona.

Some hazards are completely unexpected.

Arriving at the Milntown jump in 2006 I knew exactly where I wanted to be. But there was a rotting dead black cat covered in flies, right on the piece of wall I wanted to lean on. I couldn't bring myself to touch it, so that shot was out of the question that day. I think the best TT photos must have two or three key elements: dramatic action, crowds of spectators and scenic backgrounds. I have chosen the selection on the following pages covering the last 25 plus years mainly because every one means something to me. A few shots are quite well known, some are not, and in some cases they simply capture great moments in TT history.

Bruce Anstey threads his Suzuki through the scenery near Windy Corner in 2002.

Joey Dunlop looks nervous as he talks to Rothmans Honda team boss Barry Symmons on the start line before the 1985 Lightweight race. Joey was one of my few real heroes and so unassuming. In those days you didn't have to jostle with dozens of other photographers at the start.

Symmons recalls that chilled fuel in the RS250's tank warmed up, expanded and leaked from the breather, threatening to get on the tyres. "You were never nervous around Joey – he didn't like that." Fuel was a deciding factor in this six-lapper when race leader Brian Reid's Yamaha ran out two miles from the flag and Joey took victory. This was Joey's first 250cc TT win and the sixth of his unrivalled all-classes total of 26. It was Honda's first TT win with a two-stroke engine and the factory's first 250cc Lightweight victory since 1967.

An early black and white view of the old Grandstand in 1985. Anyone who remembers when two-strokes raced on the Mountain Course will be able to imagine the smell of burnt oil that accompanied this push-start of the 1985 Lightweight.

Erected in 1926, the old grandstand was demolished in the winter of 1985-1986 to be replaced by the present structure which stands further back from Glencrutchery Road. In this race riders were despatched in pairs but in recent years all races have had individual starting at 10-second intervals.

I was looking for wheelie shots at the start of the 1994 Formula 1 race, re-run on Sunday after Saturday's race was abandoned in a downpour. This was by far the most spectacular getaway, by Nick Jefferies on the 1000cc Britten.

The thundering Britten twins, hand-built by brilliant New Zealander John Britten, caused a stir that year but their debut was marred by team rider Mark Farmer's fatal accident in practice. In this race, the Britten suffered electrical problems. Britten, a creative engineering genius, died prematurely from skin cancer in 1995. His potent twins, with radical minimal chassis had been successful at several events around the world.

Fearless Joey Dunlop holds his 250cc Honda flat out through St Ninian's crossroads, immediately preceding the Bray Hill descent. I've taken many shots at this point but this one from 1996 has to be one of the best. The rear tyre is just off the road and there is intense concentration in Joey's eyes.

Joey, King of the Mountain is on his way to his 20th TT win in the 1996 Lightweight race on a Honda Britain two-stroke V-twin. Phillip McCallen led for two of the four laps, but slowed after bashing his Honda's exhaust system down too hard on the road. He was pushed back to third place by hard-charging Jim Moodie, also on a Honda.

Ian Simpson shoots over the brink of Bray Hill, a sensation often compared to riding off the end of the world. He had just recovered from an almighty 'tank-slapper' wobble so violent that it dislodged his right foot off the peg.

This is 1998, when Simpson won both the Formula 1 and Senior races for Honda, a fitting climax to the company's 50th anniversary celebrations held at the TT. A Scots rider whose father was a successful TT racer in the Seventies, 'Simmo' had previously won the 1997 600cc Junior race.

A carefully planned shot on Bray Hill was nearly ruined here. I never barge into residents' front gardens and had asked in advance to be in this one. But when I came back only minutes before the start of the race, two young lads were sitting right where I wanted to be. Fortunately I was able to cajole them into moving to the right and I think this photo of Ian Hutchinson is better for having them in. My original idea was to show the crowd on the other side of the road, but they are too far away. A negative situation turned into a positive one.

A shot from the 2006 Superbike race, in which 26 year old rising TT star Hutchinson, 'the Bingley Bullet' rode a McAdoo Kawasaki. He finished third behind John McGuinness and Ian Lougher (both on Hondas) in a fast, sun-blessed race. Hutchy's 2006 road racing season included wins at the North West 200 and the Ulster GP in Ireland, lapping at a record 130.828mph in the latter.

This shot of Steve Plater at the top of Bray Hill is my favourite from 2009. I tried this angle in 2004, but in recent years bikes have been going faster through St Ninian's crossroads than ever before. Bray is an unforgiving section, with a jump and wheelie at the crossroads then less than two seconds before this less well known but tricky apex before the plunge to the bottom of the hill. Steve told me he finds it okay on a flying lap but more worrying from a standing start. He seems to have a different line from others, closer to the right-hand kerb, which could be why he seems to be the only rider who gets airborne here.

Arriving at his first TT as an experienced professional racer, Plater put up an excellent debut performance in 2007 gaining a Silver Replica in all his four races. A 2008 Supersport victory came when another rider was excluded and his 2009 Senior win came after HM Plant Honda team-mate John McGuinness retired when leading. But there is no doubt that Plater is one of the Mountain Masters.

This was a case of being gifted something unusual by sheer chance. The huge cloud kicked up by Jason Griffiths' wheels came from cement dust laid to soak up oil spilled from a vehicle before the roads closed. The first few starters seemed to miss it but he fired his R1 smack down the whole line, leaving swirling grey turbulence in his wake.

The race is the 2004 Formula 1 and Griffiths finished fourth on his 1000cc Yamaha. The winner was similarly-mounted John McGuinness, who hoisted the outright Course record to a sizzling 127.68mph on his first lap. A tidy rider with many high TT finishes but no wins, Welsh-born Griffiths collected two third places and two fourths in 2004.

The master at work on Ago's leap in 1985. Joey Dunlop has the front wheel of his Honda RS250R kicked up so high that his view of the road ahead must be obscured. He kept it up like that for another couple of hundred yards as he sped towards Quarterbridge.

Dunlop didn't let a shipwreck en route to the TT from Ireland faze him in 1985. Matching Mike Hailwood's 1961 achievement, he took three wins and raised the absolute lap record to 113.95mph. Ago's Leap got its name after photographer Nick Nicholls took dramatic wheelie shots of Giacomo Agostini on his MV Agusta here in 1971. The Italian star won 10 TTs between 1966 and 1972.

Ago's Leap became a positively frightening place to watch and always attracted pass-holding photographers. This is popular Klaus Klein in 1986 practice. In the following winter, this stretch of road was partially flattened by resurfacing but it is still a fearsome place to watch from. An anecdote links Klein with Dunlop. On the eve of an early morning practice, the German was enjoying a late night drink with Joey and determined to match his pace. Only when Klaus was really worse for wear did the Irishman reveal that he was giving the next practice session a miss.

From the Stuttgart area, Klein raced at the TT from 1981 to 1987, his best result being fourth in the 1984 Classic on a 500cc Suzuki two-stroke. He died after crashing in the wet 1987 Ulster Grand Prix.

This is 1982, the first year I had a decent camera. I was using black and white film which I developed myself. I always admired Jock Taylor and his passenger Benga Johanssen, who seemed more professional and glamorous than typical Sidecar TT racers. Here they are at at Quarterbridge during an early morning practice. This slow and rather boring corner is often used by press photographers short of time, or possibly imagination. I never shoot from there now.

John 'Jock' Taylor won his last Sidecar TT, the 1982 second leg, with a best lap of 108.29mph on his 750cc Fowler Yamaha two-stroke, a record that stood for seven years. In the first leg, machine problems had forced him back to a lowly 18th place. The popular Scottish driver, Sidecar world champion with Benga in 1980, was killed racing in the 1982 Finnish Grand Prix.

Three of the fastest riders accelerate out of Quarterbridge towards Braddan Bridge in the 2004 600cc Production race. I took this with a long 600mm lens, standing in the slip-road at Braddan with trees and a spectator out of focus in the foreground. It's a heavy bazooka of a lens which always attracts attention from spectators, but worth it for a perspective that can't be achieved any other way.

The riders are John McGuinness (Yamaha) leading Ian Lougher (Honda) and Adrian Archibald (Suzuki) who kept close formation in the early stages of an exciting three-lapper. Although McGuinness (Number 3) was first to finish, the winner was Number 6 Ryan Farquhar (Kawasaki). On corrected time McGuinness was third behind Bruce Anstey (Suzuki).

A sequence I caught of Nigel Davies crashing on the entry to Braddan Bridge during a 1997 practice when the rear tyre of his fiery Yamaha YZR500 grand prix two-stroke broke away. Luckily it was the first TT where I had the advantage of an auto-focus camera and a couple of these photos were the first I had published in Motor Cycle News. Not the most tasteful way to further my career perhaps, but that's press photography and fortunately Nigel was not badly injured.

Leg injuries sustained in this prang sidelined Davies from the 1997 TT. The Welshman, nicknamed Cap returned in 1998 to finish a brilliant second in the 1000cc Production race on a Kawasaki ZX9R.

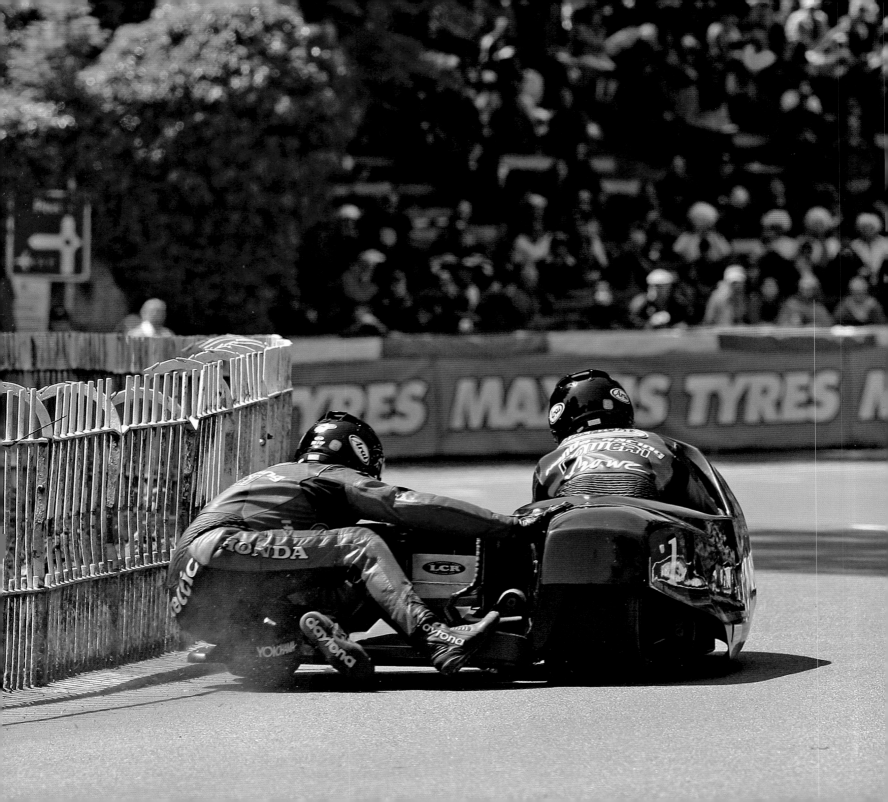

Taken one minute into the first 2009 Sidecar race, this shows Nick Crowe and his passenger Mark Cox already well in the groove, kicking up stones and grit as they skirt the railings at Braddan Bridge on their Honda outfit.

Sidecar lap record holder at 116.667mph and favourite to win, Crowe retired with a wrecked engine and fellow Manxman Dave Molyneux took his 14th win. The second race promised a showdown, but terrible misfortune struck Crowe and Cox on their first lap, when a hare ran under their rear wheel, causing the outfit to loop and catch fire. The race was abandoned and both men suffered serious injuries. Former F2 Sidecar British champion Crowe, who lost part of his right arm, now runs his own Sidecar race team.

Nigel Rollason, winner of the 1986 Sidecar Race 2, at Braddan. Passenger Donny Williams is hanging right out to keep the sidecar wheel down, something we don't see with stable modern F2 outfits. This was one of my first successful photos using colour slide film, which offers very little latitude for correct exposure.

Winner of the 1971 Senior Manx Grand Prix, Rollason graduated to the TT, first on solos and then Sidecars from 1975. His best year was 1986, when he won the second race at 103.81mph using a 750cc Barton Phoenix two-stroke engine. It originally powered the Silver Dream Racer in the 1979 movie of the same name, starring David Essex as a grand prix star in the Barry Sheene mould. After his career on wheels Rollason took up ocean yacht racing.

Jim Moodie emerges from shade as he sweeps though the right-hand bend that begins the fast and tricky Union Mills section. I took this from a place where it is (quite sensibly) forbidden to stand now.

Scot Jim Moodie put intense thought and discipline into TT riding. This is 1999, when he was a Honda team member and raised the lap record to 124.45mph in the Senior race before his rear tyre disintegrated.

Michael Rutter tips into the left-hander at Union Mills ahead of Ian Simpson in 1997 practice. Both riders were with the Honda Britain team on 750cc RC45s prepared by V&M (Valentine & Mellor).

Rutter, son of eight-times TT winner Tony Rutter, finished second behind Honda-mounted Phillip McCallen in the Formula 1 race. Simpson was third in the Senior behind McCallen's RC45 and fastest-lapper Jim Moodie's Honda NSR500V two-stroke.

This tricky Union Mills left-hander always provided a nice shot, hopping the front wheel up with a bike well cranked over. During 2001, when there was no TT due to foot and mouth disease, the bridge on the busy Douglas to Peel main road seemed to develop more of a hump, just noticeable at 30 mph in a car. I made a note to return for the last part of the 2002 Senior TT and wasn't disappointed. Ian Lougher himself didn't realise he was fully airborne here until he came across this picture in a magazine. Since then it has become one of the most photographed places, but as Ian says "We were the first!"

Lougher was second in this race behind David Jefferies, both riding TAS Suzuki GSX-R 1000s and both averaging over 124mph. Welsh-born road racing specialist Lougher has collected nine TT wins and an amazing 26 podium places.

David Jefferies swoops through Union Mills on his TAS Suzuki GSX-R1000 during the 2003 Thursday afternoon practice. On the lap after this one, DJ crashed in Crosby village and was killed instantly. Like everyone else involved with the races I was stunned with sadness.

Son of two-times TT winner Tony Jefferies and nephew of 1993 Formula 1 winner Nick Jefferies, David Jefferies was phenomenally talented and hugely popular with TT fans. A solidly-built and cheery Yorkshireman, he had a fantastic run of Mountain Course successes, winning three TTs in a week at three consecutive meetings from 1999 to 2002.

Kenny Howles and Doug Jewell silhouetted by the evening sun as they power through a swarm of mayflies at Union Mills on a Yamaha-powered outfit in 1997.

The Howells-Jewell team were fifth in the 1997 Sidecar A race, but did not finish the second event. Kenny Howells first raced at the TT in 1985 and was aggregate Sidecar winner in 1987. In 1998 his passenger was future star Sidecar pilot Nick Crowe.

This is the fast section through the built-up area of Crosby village. The rider is Jim Moodie in 1996, the year he fixed up an 11th hour ride on a Team Reve Kawasaki ridden by John Reynolds in World Superbikes. Where I was positioned, I could feel the incredible wind rush from the passing bikes, ridden flat to the stop.

Moodie won the Singles TT in 1996 but his Kawasaki rides were jinxed by a puncture that dropped him to 15th in the Formula 1 race, while ignition failure eliminated him from the Senior.

I wanted to take pictures showing the Crosby Pub as it always attracts a large crowd on a sunny race day. The bikes are really flying as they go past, towards the crest where they leap getting fully airborne before starting the downhill plunge past the Highlander, once a landmark pub.

The rider is Ian Hutchinson and this was his big moment in 2007, when collected his first TT win as the HM Plant Honda team's sole rider in the Supersport race.

How not to take Greeba Castle. Chris Heath takes corrective action after mounting the chamfered kerb on the inside of the sweeping right-hander. It's a miracle that he didn't come off.

The year is 1997 and Heath is practising on his 600cc Junior Honda on which he finished 13th in the race. He first rode the Mountain Course in 1995 and won the Open Class of the 2009 TTXGP low-emissions race on an electric-powered machine.

A rear shot of Cameron Donald exiting Greeba Castle on a TAS Suzuki in 2008 practice. Light conditions at Greeba Castle are always a gamble and can change between the roads closing and the first machine arriving. Low evening sunlight is essential for that golden glow in the tree canopy.

Donald made a meteoric move from being a plumber in Melbourne, Australia to TT stardom. In 2006, only his second year on the Island, he finished second in the Senior with a fantastic 128mph-plus lap on a Honda. Missing 2007 through an injury sustained racing in Ireland, he was back in the groove in 2008, winning both the Superbike and Superstock TTs on TAS Suzukis.

Paul Hunt at Appledene, against the dark backdrop created by trees on this section after Greeba Castle.

Taken in 2005 practice. Retired from racing, Hunt is now a TT Travelling Marshal.

Evening sun illuminates Michael Dunlop's eyes as he powers out of Greeba Bridge in 2009 practice.

Son of Robert and nephew of Joey, Dunlop won the Supersport 2 race on this Yamaha.

This location opposite the Hawthorn Pub is difficult to reach.

Cameron Donald and Conor Cummins in 2009 practice.

Richard 'Milky' Quayle (Honda) at Ballacraine in the 2002 400cc Supersport race he won.

This was the first TT win by a Manx rider for 35 years.

Maybe that's why his friends call him 'Scratch'? Northern Irish rider Adrian Archibald makes sparks fly cranking round the sharp right at Ballacraine.

Archibald led the 2005 Superstock race and set a new lap record at 126.64mph before running out of fuel only six miles from the chequered flag and handing victory to his TAS Suzuki team-mate Bruce Anstey. Now a furniture shop, the building in the background was the Ballacraine pub until the mid-Eighties.

Bruce Anstey at Ballaspur. Spectating is no longer allowed here.

This is the 2004 Senior in which Anstey finished second.

These two shots across the River Neb at Black Dub are 15 years apart. After I took the first of 1992 Sidecar double winner Geoff Bell (left), a bush grew up to block the view. After it was cut down I took the second of Steve Norbury in 2007.

Bell drives a Yamaha outfit passengered by Keith Cornbill and the ballast on Norbury's Lockside Yamaha is Scott Parnell. Steve Norbury was killed racing in Germany during 2008.

Previous Page Left: Cameron Donald at Lambfell, where the Cronk-y-Voddy straight begins, in 2009 Wednesday practice. In Thursday's session his second flying lap was at 131mph, an unofficial outright record. Too bad that he fell off after taking to the grass at Keppel Gate on the Friday night and put himself out of the races with shoulder and back injuries. He told me later that he was on an 'easy' lap to bed the bike in for the race and might not have been focusing hard enough.

Winner of two TTs in 2008, Donald's sensational fastest 2009 practice lap was at 131.457mph, while Relentless by TAS Suzuki team-mate Bruce Anstey recorded his first 130mph lap in practice.

Previous Page Right: Guy Martin banks into a leftward kink at the end of the Cronk-y-Voddy straight. I took this from private property, with permission, but didn't want to stay long. Photos don't do justice to the speed at which they go through here.

Likeable Guy Martin was one of the most talked about riders in 2006. Clearly on the brink of stardom, he was very open in press interviews and not afraid to talk about the TT's dangers. Disappointing results were put down to machine problems and he failed to finish in this race.

In 1998 I got permission to stand above the high stone wall on the inside of the right-hander at the Handley's Corner S-bends. This photo of Nigel Piercy is one of the better results, but I didn't find this angle as interesting as I had envisaged.

Nigel Piercy finished 15th on his Mannin Collections/TSB Honda in the 1998 Ultra lightweight race, shortened to from four laps to three by bad weather.

A very hazardous location to photograph from, if a bike lost control it doesn't bear thinking about, certainly I wouldn't go back. Even in a car on open roads Handleys is intimidating: as you approach, that Manx stone wall looms bigger and bigger. I don't think I could improve on this 2005 picture: I just pressed a button and John McGuinness provided the drama. Look at the courage and commitment in those eyes, no wonder that he's the man to beat.

Another angle on the top of Barregarrow, an incredibly fast left kink. Here Steve Cull (4) chases Johnny Rea, both on Yamahas, in the 1990 600cc Supersport. It looks as though Cull's tyre is pattering slightly at well over 100mph – rather him than me. Rea is out of focus, but for me that doesn't detract from this picture.

These two riders finished the race in this order, taking second and third places behind winner Brian Reid: a 1-2-3 for Ulstermen. Johnny Rea, father of World Superbikes star Jonathan Rea, rode in the TT from 1983 to 1994 and won the 1989 350cc Junior.

David Jefferies whistles past the old church at the top of Barregarrow hill in the 2000 Junior race. There is a saying that good TT riders don't look quick, but DJ never looked anything else and had a style all of his own. He had could grab any bike by the scruff of the neck and bully it into submission.

Winning this Junior race on his 600cc V&M Yamaha meant that 'big David' Jefferies had achieved TT success in every class he'd competed in. It was also a breakthrough for Yamaha, as Honda had won every 600cc Junior since it was first run in 1995.

Out of the seat, Dave Leach sends sparks flying as he scrapes through the bottom of Barregarrow in the 1989 750cc Production race. Modern machines with higher exhaust pipes rarely make sparks. Note the spectators on the right, now a strictly prohibited area. After being lost for seven years, this photo was recently retrieved from a magazine's files. Endless perfect copies can be made of digital images but with transparency film mislaying the original is a disaster.

In this race Leach finished second, sandwiched between the Honda RC30s of winner Carl Fogarty and Steve Hislop. Two days later he would win the 1300cc Production race, an event overshadowed by the death of two top riders Phil Mellor and Steve Henshaw. Dave Leach collected four TT wins in between 1988 and 1991.

The bottom of the Barregarrow hill, with a blind left kink by Ivie Cottage and its prominent chimney stack, is a real test of nerve. A dust cloud puffs from Steve Plater's Yamaha as his tyre picks up pulverised glass fibre from the fairing's belly pan as it smashes onto the tarmac. It may look as though I took this standing on the course, but I'm actually stood behind a low bridge wall.

This was consummate professional Plater's first year at the TT in 2007, when he learned the roads rapidly and collected silver replicas in all four of his races. His best performance was in the Senior, finishing seventh and averaging 123.076mph for six laps.

Trees dwarf a bike as it approaches Douglas Road corner, at the entry to Kirk Michael. Two-times winner Ia *Duffus on a 600cc Yamaha in 2003, his last year at the TT.*

Tucked away on his 125cc Honda, Robert Dunlop passes the crowd watching from the car park of the Mitre *in Kirk Michael village, 1997.*

Passed fit for the 1997 TT, even though he was still unable to race in Ireland because of partial disablem from crash injuries, Joey Dunlop's brother Robert stuck with the smallest Ultra Lightweight class and too third place.

Spectators relax outside the Mitre pub at Kirk Michael in the evening sun as Guy Martin flies through the be *on his Hydrex Honda. I stood in the garden of a house opposite and caught this when the two guys leaning* *the wall were looking interested in the action. At times they weren't, but you can only go so far in trying to dir* *complete strangers from the other side of the road.*

Martin is seen here in 2009's Friday evening practice. He gained excellent results in his fifth TT, finishing second in the Superstock and Supersport 1 races and third in the Superbike, but not the win he desperately wanted. A broken drive chain in the Senior added to his frustration.

Left: *Passing the bank, the shops, the post office and the church, Joey Dunlop holds full throttle through Kirk Michael village on his Honda in the 2000 125cc race (shame about that ugly orange litter bin). Joey's confident riding gave him a historic third hat-trick of three TT wins and in a masterful piece of understatement he told the press after the third: " It seems to be a good week". What a star!*

This victory on a Honda RS125 would be Dunlop's incredible 26th in the TT. He won by 16 seconds from Denis McCullough, with younger brother Robert Dunlop third. It would be the King of the Mountain's last TT: he was killed racing a 125cc in Estonia in July 2000.

Owen McNally (Aprilia) cresting the jump at the start of the spectacular Rhencullen section in the 1999 250cc Lightweight.

One of Ireland's best road racers with three North West 200 wins to his name, McNally from Coleraine contested the TT from 1995 to 1999, achieving two top-three rostrum finishes in 125cc races. He died after crashing at the Ulster Grand Prix in August 1999.

Who is braver, the rider or the spectators? Most photos of this jump are taken from the other side of the road where the huge crowd is. There was nowhere more exhilarating to watch as bikes headed straight for them, their front wheels pointing skywards. Then, just when it seemed too late, the front tyre would kiss the road and the bike could be flung into the right-hand kink preceding the Birkin's Bend left sweep. This is Brian Reid in the 1993 250cc race.

Ulsterman Brian Reid took his fifth TT win in this Junior race. Riding a Yamaha he fended off Honda riders Jim Moodie, who finished second, and third placeman Joey Dunlop. Joey's brother Robert set the fastest lap on a Yamaha at 116.75mph.

Above: *Iain Duffus being chased by Joey Dunlop through Rhencullen in the 1995 250cc Lightweight race. The 30mph limit sign adds a touch of irony, but what a shame it had to acquire that hideous yellow surround in the mid-Nineties.*

In his 20th year of TT racing, Dunlop won on his Honda with a new lap record at 117.57mph and a record four-lap average of115.68mph average. Duffus did not finish on his Yamaha.

Left: *At Rhencullen for the 2007 Superbike race, someone told me to look out for Number 23 (James McBride), who was crossed-up like this on every lap. It's a miracle he never crashed. He told me later he had a rear suspension problem in this race.*

James McBride from Kettering was clearly a rising TT star in 2007 but during practice in 2008 he fell off at the 160mph Gorse Lea curve and sustained serious fractures.

The jump in the final part of the Rhencullen section lifts Steve Henshaw's Suzuki RG500 off in the 1988 Senior race. This was taken when I changed to Kodachrome colour slide film, with a 64 ASA rating demanding slower shutter speeds.

Nottinghamshire TT regular Henshaw did not finish this fast and furious race, won by Joey Dunlop. Badly injured in a 1984 practice accident, he recovered but did not survive a crash in the 1989 1300cc Production race.

Left: *Typical head-down style by Phil McCallen as he drives out of the Rhencullen section on a Production Honda in 1997.*

This was McCallen's second consecutive win in the Production race, reintroduced for 1996. He rode a CBR900RR FireBlade sponsored by the Motorcycle City dealer chain in both events. The 1997 race, shortened to two laps because of the weather, was one of his three wins in a TT that also saw him walk away from a high-speed fall from his 250cc machine.

With just a patch of his rear tyre on the road, Adrian Archibald leaves Rhencullen on his TAS Suzuki to dive under the trees past Bishop's Court at 150mph-plus. John McGuinness gave me the tip that the outrageously powerful Superbikes loft the front wheel here and in several other new places.

The year is 2006, when former bicycle racer and three-times TT winner Archibald had an off year. He finished a lowly 13th in this Senior race.

Page 63 Top: *Ballaugh Bridge is the most photographed point on the Course. Getting something different here is a challenge, which is why I took this 1992 Formula 1 shot of Trevor Nation with the camera down at road level, looking up.*

Nation's TT career stretched from 1980 to 1995, with production race wins in 1984 and 1986 plus second place in the 1990 Senior on a Norton. In this race, he finished eighth on the Ducati 888 V-twin.

Page 63 Below: *Dave Molyneux and passenger Dan Sayle get airborne on the Bridge. Taken from a front garden in Ballaugh Village, this head-on angle gives the impression that Moly is looking straight at the camera, something you can't get from the more usual closer position.*

This is 2005, when Manx sidecar maestro Molyneux won Sidecar race B and raised the lap record to 116.04mph on his self-built Honda-engined DMR outfit.

Left ,on Page 62: *Wayde Boyd may not be among the fastest riders, but he could be the highest jumper on Ballaugh Bridge. Some riders avoid attacking the hump-back in motocross style as it adds to wear on chains and sprockets.*

Colourful Wade Boyd from San Francisco rode in the TT from 1992 to 2007, following his father Billy who raced once in 1966. In this 2003 Formula 1 race he finished 36th on a Kawasaki.

Left: *Almost brushing the wall by the Raven pub, Steve Cull flies through Ballaugh on his Suzuki RG500 in the 1985 Senior race. The spectator standing on the railings was asked to move by a marshal, in the most polite way: "Excuse me sir, I don't want to spoil your enjoyment but …"   or words to that effect.*

Sixth in this race, Cull had finished second in the Junior on a Yamaha two days earlier. In a TT career from 1976 to 1991 he notched up two wins and pushed the absolute lap record at 119.08mph in the 1988 Senior before his Honda RS500 caught fire.

Right: *Spray is thrown up from the rear tyre of Joey Dunlop's Honda at Ballaugh in the 1998 250cc TT.*

Gritty Dunlop won this shortened wet race despite pain from injuries sustained earlier in the season. It was his 23rd TT victory

Left: *Leaves are lying on the road as Adrian Archibald goes through on the first lap of the 2003 Formula 1, started late due to the weather.*

In a race overshadowed by the absence of David Jefferies, his TAS Suzuki team mate Archibald took a win from Ian Lougher (Honda SP-2) and John McGuinness (Ducati)

After tearing back by car from the Ballacrye jump half a mile away, I got to Ballaugh Bridge in time to catch this historic shot of Steve Hislop on his last ever TT racing lap in the 1994 Senior race. A true legend, Hizzy was most naturally gifted TT rider I've ever seen.

Hugely popular Hislop moved away from TT racing after his 1992 Senior win, but returned for a final appearance with the Castrol Honda team in 1994. Wins in the Formula 1 and Senior took his total of TT victories to 11.

Previous page: *I'd planned this 1997 Ballacrye shot months ahead, to capture a bike rear-on and show how fans were flocking to this newly-discovered viewpoint. Rushing here from Sulby Bridge I wanted to catch the leader Phillip McCallen. I knew he ran close to the white line and with a nod from the marshal I dashed across the road. With dozens of spectators soaking up the sunny weather, everything seemed to be in place. But just as I heard McCallen banging up through the gears as he left Ballaugh I realised the view was blocked by a bush that had grown since my last visit. I felt a blast of wind as the Honda screamed past my left shoulder, and knowing it was at least 20 seconds ahead of the next bike, I leaned into the road just as the RC45's engine note shot up when the back tyre lost traction. I rattled off two frames before quickly retreating into the field. That bike was too close for comfort and on reflection I must say that no picture is worth risking an accident for.*

Always alarming to watch, McCallen won three TTs in 1997 taking his total to 11 before an early-season back injury in 1998 ended his extraordinary run of Mountain Course successes.

Right: *The Ballacrye leap, as taken by Carl Fogarty in his epic 1992 Senior battle with Steve Hislop.*

In this race Fogarty (Loctite Yamaha) set an outright lap record at 123.61mph, which would stand for seven years. But the win went to arch-rival Steve Hislop, riding heroically on a Norton Rotary.

Far Right: *Conor Cummins is right out of the seat going over a bump as he passes the Sulby Glen pub. Unable to tuck his tall frame away on his Supersport McAdoo Kawasaki, he goes down the following Sulby Straight at 180mph-plus sitting on the tail fairing behind the seat, so as to keep his head down behind the screen.*

This is 2009 when Ramsey resident Cummins became the Isle of Man's fastest TT rider with a 130mph lap on his way to second place in the 2009 Senior. He was third in this race, the Supersport 1.

Braking hard at the end of Sulby straight, ready for the right-hander at the Bridge.

Eventual winner Jim Moodie heads fellow Scot Iain Duffus in the 1993 600cc Supersport race.

Tony Rutter rode with an effortless and elegant style that shows clearly in this shot of him rounding Sulby Bridge on his Formula 2 Ducati. Look at the legs dangling over that wall: a bygone era!

Ducati factory rider Rutter was reigning F2 world champion when he won this 1985 race, his seventh and last TT victory. His son Michael won the 1998 Junior TT..

The famous Ginger Hall pub just along from Sulby Bridge offers a great view of the deceptive left-hander, with refreshments on tap. A sizeable crowd watches this close battle between Brian Morrison (left) and Phil McCallen in the 1990 Formula 1 race.

Morrison finished fourth in this race on his Honda RC30, while similarly-mounted McCallen was a lowly 39th after stopping for 15 minutes at the pits to fix a carburettor linkage problem. The winner was Carl Fogarty, also on one of the Honda V4s.

An elevated view of Sulby Bridge and the Ginger Hall beyond. My previous year's plan to use a 30ft hoist was dashed by adverse weather, but in 1999 I managed it. Conditions were perfect for this Sidecar Race B, unless you were on the tea tray-sized platform of a 'cherry picker' not really intended for outdoor use! A Motor Cycle News staff photographer begged me to let him use it: after the trouble I had gone to, like no way Howard!

The outfit is driven by Cumbrian driver Rob Fisher with Rick Long as passenger. They won this race on a Baker Yamaha after leader and Race A winner Dave Molyneux retired on the last lap.

Above: *A sidecar duel at Ginger Hall in 1995 with Rob Fisher and Boyd Hutchinson leading veteran competitors Mick Boddice and Dave Wells. I held the camera low to the ground at the end of the railings.*

Fisher won both Sidecar races in 1995, despite an accident in Thursday's practice and raised the lap record to 107.58mph.

Iron railings run along the inside of the left-hander overlooked by the Ginger Hall. Jim Moodie is keeping well clear of them in this 1997 photo, but concerns that riders might catch their helmets on the ironwork led to part of the railings being covered by wooden boards in recent years.

In this Formula 1 race, Moodie's 750cc Crescent Suzuki failed to last. But in the Senior he rode a Padgett Honda RS500V two-stroke to finish second to Phillip McCallen's Honda RC45 and set the fastest lap at 124.45mph.

This angle shows the famous pub's frontage and the crowd, as well as a telegraph pole close to the road.

The riders are Guy Martin (15) and Rob Frost, both on 600cc Supersport Hondas in 2005

Below: *In this 1990 photo from the Formula 1 race, the front tyre of Robert Dunlop's Norton skips over a treacherous ripple which has since been ironed out by road resurfacing.*

Fresh from two wins in Ireland's North West 200 on the unorthodox Rotary-engined John Player Norton, Dunlop finished third. In 1991 he collected another third place for Norton, after over-heating ended his Formula 1 charge.

Milntown, on the approach to Ramsey, is not a place to watch for the faint-hearted. Flying off the slightly humped bridge over the Auldyn river, riders then follow the road as it curves to the right, skimming a stone wall on the inside. Here I caught Joey Dunlop leaping in the 1991 Senior.

Dunlop finished second to Steve Hislop, both riding factory Honda RVF750s

I chose this 1993 shot of Nick Jefferies from many similar photos at Glentramman purely for the quality of light. Sunlight reflecting off the tank may have only last a split second but it illuminated intense concentration on Nick's face behind his dark visor. Pure luck.

Jefferies, whose older brother Tony won two TTs and nephew David won nine, took his sole victory in this Formula 1 race on a Honda RC30. Having previously won in a Manx Grand Prix in 1983 race and the 1976 Manx Two-Day Trial, he achieved a unique hat-trick.

Left: Another Milntown view, with MV Agusta-mounted Martin Finnegan, on his way to fourth place in the 2007 Superstock. He was a favourite for me, spectacular on the bike yet so unassuming off it. The signpost adds to the composition here, but roadsigns can block potentially great shots.

Irish rider Finnegan gave the Italian MV marque its best TT result for 35 years. He had nine top-six finishes including third place in the 2005 Superbike TT, but was killed racing on the Tandragee circuit in 2008.

The right-hander immediately after the Milntown jump is bumpy but very quick, with a stone wall on the inside and no kerb. This is Keith Amor aiming his CBR600 down the straight leading towards Ramsey in 2008.

Scots rider Amor grasped the challenge of TT racing in 2007 and learned fast, collecting third place in this Supersport race the following year. Two more podium places in 2009 confirmed him as one of the new generation of TT stars.

I make a point of almost never taking a photograph at normal eye level. It is always better to be high up or kneeling at gutter level. Keeping the camera low to the road paid off here: you can see how hard Nick Crowe is pushing his outfit through White Gates, the low angle and heat haze adds to the impact of the wheel skipping off the tarmac.

A Sidecar passenger before becoming a driver, Nick Crowe ended a run of non-finishes in 2003 with two second places, one behind fellow Manxman Dave Molyneux. In this 2004 race Crowe and passenger Darren Hope had to settle for being runners-up behind Moly again, but victory would come in the following year.

A trio of 750cc Honda RC45s crest May Hill on the road out of Ramsey in the 1998 Senior, finale to the Honda company's 50th anniversary celebrations. Eventual winner Ian Simpson begins peeling off for the White Gates left-hander ahead of James Courtney and Michael Rutter.

In this eventful finale to 1998, Rutter took an early lead, his opening lap at 123.04mph being the best in the race. Slowed by a flat tyre before reaching the flag, he finished second with Courtney third.

Joey Dunlop at Ramsey Hairpin on the way to his fantastic TT victory in the 2000 Formula 1 race, an event he won six times in a row earlier in his career. Just to keep us photographers on our toes, his Honda SP-1 changed colour from blue and purple Vimto livery to Honda Britain red between practice and the race. Photographers all round the course must have groaned in unison when they heard this on the radio commentary. Any practice shots of Joey on the SP1 suddenly looked useless. But when he came out again for the Senior it had been changed back. If you get caught out by something like that, you can miss vital shots. I nearly missed this one grabbing a photo of the signal being given to thirsty Joey.

In 2000, Dunlop was 48 and had not won a TT on an over-250cc machine for five years. The Formula 1 was his first TT on a Honda VTR1000 SP-1 V-twin, upgraded to full World Superbikes specification to make it competitive against fours. He took an early lead on tricky dry and damp roads, only being challenged by David Jefferies who led briefly before his clutch failed. Joey went on to win two more races, the 250cc and 125cc TTs, taking his total to 26. He was killed competing at a minor meeting in Tallin, Estonia a few weeks later.

Far Left: *A classic leafy Gooseneck view of Robert Dunlop during the 2003 Ultra Lightweight TT, the gorse flowers complementing the yellow Honda.*

Dunlop finished fourth in this race, the last 125cc TT race run on the Mountain Course. It was won by Chris Palmer, who had moved from his home in Cumbria to live on the Island.

Couldn't resist this one, but I must stress that I took it during an unusually long race postponement in 2003 when the roads stayed closed and there was nothing to do for hours.

This flag marshals' shelter is on the approach to the Gooseneck. The green and white tubs contain absorbent powder to put on fluid spills. The portable radio set will be tuned to Radio TT on AM to catch the latest information.

Overleaf: *Motor sport photographers use long telephoto lenses to get as close to the subject as possible, but magnificent scenic views like this at the Gooseneck on the Mountain climb are best captured with a wider angled lens. The Sidecar is being driven by Dave Molyneux with passenger Karl Ellison putting his weight over the rear wheel as they slew round the sharp uphill right-hander.*

This is 1993, the year 'Moly' won his first Sidecar TT double, an achievement he would repeat three more times. Using a Yamaha engine, he set a new lap record at 104.27mph in Race A.

Previous Page Left: My favourite shot of David Jefferies, typically playing to the crowd as he exits the Gooseneck on the rear wheel of his V&M Yamaha R1 in 1999 practice.

Jefferies took a trio of 1999 wins on V&M Yamahas, in the Formula 1, 1000cc Production and Senior races. In 2000 he made it a double hat-trick with wins in the 600cc Junior, 1000cc Production and the Senior, with a scorching record lap at 125.69mph in the latter.

Previous Page Right: With a blaze of gorse and the deep blue of the sea in the background, Sean Harris leads Ryan Farquhar on the Mountain climb before Joey's bend, 26 miles out. Bikes are driving hard through this section - you can see them laying rubber on the road. I always make sure I have a good escape route in case of the unexpected.

After he won two Production races in 2003, much was expected of mercurial New Zealander Shaun Harris. But 2004 was an unhappy year with a 12th place his only finish in five races. Returning full of determination in 2007, he crashed at Union Mills in the Superstock race. Critically injured, he eventually recovered but has not raced again. Irishman Farquhar graduated to the TT in 2002 with two MGP victories and went on to win the 2004 600cc Production TT and the 2005 Supersport Junior B race. He's had bad luck in TTs but winning 61 Irish races in 2009 earned him the Irish Motorcyclist of the year trophy.

This is one of those shots that could really only be of the TT. Taken in 1990 it shows driver Dave Saville and passenger Nick Roche, double Sidecar TT winners that year on their Sabre outfit at the Guthrie Memorial on the Mountain Climb. Ramsey and the Island's northern plain are visible in the background. I'll admit to poaching the idea for this photograph from a Seventies' Avon tyres advertisement showing Mike Hailwood. To get the low angle I had to lie in a road drainage ditch.

Dave Saville was one of the greatest TT Sidecar pilots. A pioneer of Formula 2 machinery in their early days, he topped the class seven times when it ran within the 1000cc Sidecar race. F2 was adopted as the standard Sidecar TT Formula in 1990, when he won both races. Saville also raced solos and his career was ended by a fall in the 1993 Senior Classic MGP which left him severely disabled. Sadly, he died in 2006.

The Memorial was erected after Jimmy Guthrie, six times a TT winner, was killed racing in Germany in 1937. His native Scotland can be seen clearly from here on a clear day.

Far right: Another glorious day and another shot from Guthrie's that oozes TT atmosphere. I love backgrounds where the line of the road takes your eye into the far off distance.

The riders are Joey Dunlop (12) and Adrian Archibald, both from Ballymoney, NI. The race is the 1999 600cc Junior, in which they finish fifth and fourth respectively on Honda CBR600s.

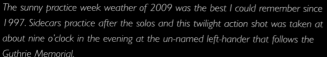

The sunny practice week weather of 2009 was the best I could remember since 1997. Sidecars practice after the solos and this twilight action shot was taken at about nine o'clock in the evening at the un-named left-hander that follows the Guthrie Memorial.

The driver is Tim Reeves, who came to the TT in 2008 after winning three world championships on short circuits, passengered by TT regular Patrick Farrance. Reeves made an excellent debut with a third and a sixth place, while they took fourth in the 2009 Sidecar Race A. (Race B was abandoned after Nick Crowe's serious first-lap crash.)

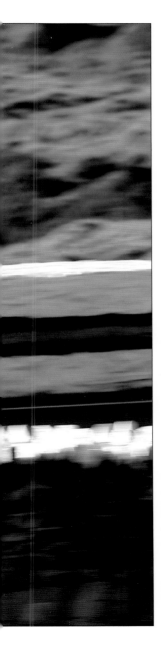

Painted white with black and yellow stripes for visibility in fog, stone culvert walls on the Mountain Road are part of TT iconography. At an early 2009 practice I decided to stand well back, on marshy ground, from this bridge over a gulley about half a mile beyond Guthrie's. It's a critical point for getting full drive onto the Mountain Mile straight. I chose this particular shot because the yellow and black of James McBride and his Yamaha match the masonry paint.

Returning to the TT after falling off at Gorse Lea in 2008, McBride finished all his five 2009 races with a respectable 16th place in the Senior.

Standing out sharply against the Mountain landscape, Denis McCullough powers his 250cc Honda round the Mountain Box right-hander in the 1999 Lightweight race

County Down rider McCullough came fourth in this event. He finished second in the 125cc TT three times between 1994 and 2000.

Above: *The unmistakeable aggressive chin-glued-to-the-tank style of Phil McCallen at Black Hut, the left-hander that starts the smooth and fast and Verandah section on the slopes of Snaefell. It is interesting to note that many of the quicker TT riders don't often drag their knees on the tarmac, short circuit-style.*

McCallen is on his 750cc Honda Britain RC45 during a 1997 evening practice. Out to improve on his record four wins in 1996, he had to settle for three after miraculously escaping injury when crashing in the Lightweight and being beaten by Ian Simpson in the 600cc Junior.

I think the single lone spectator adds atmosphere to this long lens shot of Richard Britton in 2005, where placing the bike neatly between the reflector posts was essential for the composition. It's a sobering thought that there were once concrete posts lining this remote part of the Mountain Road 400m above sea level.

This was Britton's last year in the TT, when he was fifth in the Senior and eighth in the Superstock race on DMRR Honda FireBlades. The Ulster-based rider, whose Island debut was a win in the 1997 Manx GP Junior Newcomers race, was greatly liked and respected by fellow competitors. He was killed racing at Ballybunion, Eire in October 2005.

In 2006's Wednesday evening practice John McGuinness is spinning his rear tyre, as he tips into the long sweeping right hand bends after Bungalow Bridge. It's hard for a still photograph to do justice to this fantastically fast series of bends, called the Verandah.

Joining the HM Plant Honda team as its TT ace, McGuinness rapidly got the hang of a 1000cc FireBlade road machine converted into a TT Superbike, winning both the Superbike and Senior races on it. The building in the background is an alpine-style shelter commemorating Les Graham, killed during the 1953 Senior TT.

Whenever I'm asked the best place to watch, I say head to the hills if the weather's good. On clear bright practice or race day the mountain section offers the best back drops anywhere around the course, as seen in this photo taken near the 32nd Milestone.

The rider is David Jefferies on a Suzuki GXSX-R1000, on his way to winning the 2002 Production race.

At Kate's Cottage, a blind downhill left-hander, water from a spring under the road creates a permanent wet patch, smack on the racing line. The middle photo shows Adrian Archibald hammering through the bend after riding straight through the patch in 2002. For several years I aimed to get a shot of the spray thrown up, back-lit during a sunny evening practice. I succeeded in 2007, catching McGuinness storming through a fraction too hot, only milliseconds after his Dunlop slicks have raised a flash of spray. John is feathering the front brake, which loads up the front tyre, seen squashing into the road surface.

Seen here on a Honda, Archibald joined TAS Suzuki for 2003 to win both the Formula 1 and Senior. He won the Senior again in 2004. In 2007, McGuinness won the Superbike and Senior races on his HM Plant Honda. The Senior saw him round off Centenary celebrations perfectly with the first 130mph lap.

Alan Batson hits the bank at Kate's. He was obviously running too wide and destined to make impact, but had a lucky escape and didn't even come off the machine. The rider on the right line is Ian Simpson

This happened in the 1995 Junior, the first year it was a 600cc race. Batson continued to finished 12th.

By the Creg-ny-Baa pub at the 1984 Production race, the last time I ever tried to mix photography and watching with my mates, drink in hand.

The leading 250cc Class C riders are journalist Mat Oxley, plus local stars Graham Cannell and Chris Fargher, all on Suzuki Gamma two-strokes. Cannell's bike seized on the last lap, Fargher was second behind Phil Mellor (Yamaha) and Oxley third.

From 1991's final practice. The sight of three Honda team riders approaching Brandish, lit by a late summer evening glow, was amazing. I waited anxiously for my transparencies to come back from the lab in France and when they did, this one shot I desperately wanted was under-exposed. But thanks to intensive Photoshop editing at Lily Publications I have a record of that unforgettable evening.

The rivalry between Steve Hislop (11) and Carl Fogarty (8) on their super-fast factory RVF750s electrified practice week in 1991, with both riders lapping at inane speeds. In this last practice they completed a relatively sedate lap together, followed by team-mate Nick Jefferies on his RC30 fitted with a video camera.

Middle View: *Motor sport TV pioneer Brian Kreisky working at Governor's Bridge during a 1985 practice. The rider is Swede Peter Linden on a Production Honda VF1000R. This corner, slowest on the Course, has now changed beyond recognition. Mr Kreisky was killed in a helicopter crash in 2000.*

Fighter pilot Linden, who had ridden a VF1000R to fifth place in the 1984 Le Mans 24 Hour endurance race, finished fifth in the 1985 Production TT.

Far Right: *This is the last ever morning practice session and a sombre occasion as it was the day after David Jefferies had died. Jun Maeda observes a private ritual and I kept a respectful distance so as not to interfere.*

Maeda from Kyoto, Japan first raced at the 1998 TT and worked his way up to take two top six finishes in 2005, when a lap at 124.78mph made him the 12th fastest competitor. Involved in a collision with another rider in 2006 practice, he later died from his injuries.

I was in the pits to catch the moment when Steve Hislop retired from the 1994 Formula I race, hit by torrential rain. Behind him, wet tyres are being put on Phil McCallen's bike instead of slicks so he can continue. The other finish line photo taken shortly afterwards shows the race being stopped, with 'winner' Nigel Davies first to be red-flagged.

The abandoned Formula I race was re-run on the following day, when Hislop won.

David Jefferies holds the Senior TT trophy in 2002. TAS Suzuki team principals Phillip and Hector Neill check the names of past winners.

This was TT hero DJ's ninth and last victory.

HANDS OFF

A casual remark by John McGuinness, asking me why TT photographers always seeme to shoot from the same places year after year, really got me thinking about my approach. One of my concerns was how some of the best locations were becoming no-go areas, mainly in response to fatal crashes and the ensuing publicity.

As a result, I began using remotely triggered cameras in 2007. The technology has been around since the Nineties: look behind the goal at a Premier League football match or the finish line of an Olympic 100 metres final and you'll see a multitude of cameras with remote radio triggers.

The body is mounted on an adjustable arm, which fixes to a solid roadside object such as a railing or the post for a road sign. I operate the shutter with a transmitter which has a range of up to about 100metres, so I can fire the camera from the other side of the road and occasionally appear in my own shots!

The great advantage of this method is that I can shoot from places where a photographer cannot go either because it is inaccessible or a prohibited area for safety reasons. Another attraction for me was that, to my knowledge, no-one else had used this technique at the TT before.

Remote cameras can involve laborious setting-up, but the results when I get it right are worth the extra effort. I engage in total communication and co-operation with marshals: if anything seems in any way hazardous, it isn't done.

Ian Hutchinson in the 2009 Supersport Race 2. This angle took three years to get to a point where I'm fairly happy with the result. Still room for improvement though, as my school teachers used to say. The start of this race was delayed for three hours, so my plan for full-on sun from behind the camera fell through. The remote camera can be seen firmly strapped to a traffic light pole, from where it took the shot on the left. The above photo was taken at the same moment from across the road, with the hand-held camera that triggered the remote set-up.

I wanted to show the entire backdrop of Bray Hill with all the street furniture and large crowds. Many years ago photos were taken from this angle, when bikes used to launch off a manhole cover that has thankfully been removed. In this first lap shot of the 2009 Superbike race, the suspension on Ryan Farquhar's Kawasaki with a full fuel load is bottoming-out..

Setting up for this started at 6am, four hours before the roads closed. My remote camera is clamped to a wooden fence and to avoid interference from overhanging trees I had to take up position among spectators in a garden. You can see me on the left of the picture between the traffic lights and behind a man in a bright blue shirt. Proving you can't plan enough I had even consulted with the TV company using the orange cameras seen on the kerb to be sure there was no conflict with their equipment.

Overleaf: One of my favourite remote shots, which only became possible after the junction layout at Braddan was changed between the 2008 and 2009 TTs. Both were triggered from the Church enclosure. Steve Plater, on his way to winning the 2009 Senior, has his line inch-perfect to get on throttle a tad earlier for the straight run to Union Mills. That can make the difference between lapping at 129mph and 130mph. The camera is clamped to a metal barrier that looks ugly when you shoot from the other side of the road. I politely asked the authorities if it could be painted white to make it more photogenic and got a fairly impolite 'no'.

Remote shooting with a camera clamped to a gate let me get this fresh view of the bump on the bridge at Union Mills. The rider is Jimmy Moore from Oregon, USA in his third 2009 practice session. He told me that the reason for getting so much air under his Yamaha's rear wheel was a too-stiff rear suspension setting, sorted by the end of practice.

In 2009 I was armed with three cameras and aimed to get angles never seen before, with one handheld camera and two on remote set-ups. On this balmy summer evening at Greeba Bridge I was looking for close-up views of bikes just popping their front wheels exiting the bend. Enter Spanish road test journalist Sergio Romero stage right. I have covered the TT for his magazine for several years and probably shouldn't have encouraged him to pose by telling him where I was shooting from in that practice. This was Sergio's second year at the TT, when he lapped at over 120mph on a 1000cc Kawasaki.

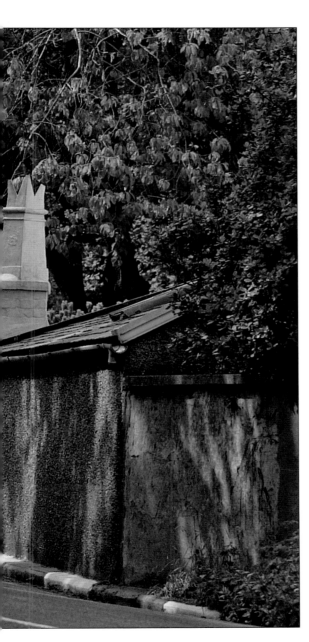

Page 120 Left: The TT as cows see it? I had visited the Lambfell area before 2009 practice week started and in overcast weather this gate didn't look anything special. But in the warm sunshine we had for practice I was struck by the flaking red paint and the way the bars framed the road and the marshals. I could have taken this hand-held, but clamping the camera to a post let me go elsewhere without being tied down. The front wheel of Guy Martin's Hydrex Honda Superbike is just lifting off the road as he winds up for the 180mph Cronk-y-Voddy straight.

Page 121 Right: After I fired the remote camera behind the gate, I took this hand-held shot of Martin about 100 yards further along the road

There is no way a photographer could stand where this shot was taken at the bottom of Barregarrow. It is of John McGuinness on his historic first 130mph lap on an HM Plant Honda in the 2007 Centenary Senior race and one of my first successful attempts at remote triggering. As the firing of a remote camera is not instantaneous, the process can be hit-and-miss.

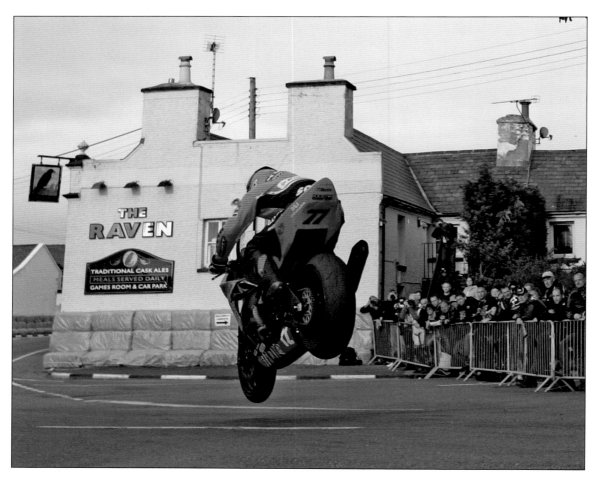

A different view of much-photographed Ballaugh Bridge, with the camera clamped to the railings so as to get an idea of the riders' perspective on the pub and spectators. These two photos were taken during the 2009 Superstock race.

I was positioned beyond the pub and out of range for the camera radio signal, so I'll come clean and admit that this shot was taken by my wife Christine who had foolishly decided to accompany me that day.

Above: Ryan Farquahar, whose positioning on the Bridge is always different from other riders', is about to make a front wheel landing on his Kawasaki..

Right: Conor Cummins (McAdoo Kawasaki) launches off the hump.

Seen from a low angle, Steve Plater follows Conor
Cummins through the right-hand kink on a culvert
above Guthrie's Memorial. A rider maintaining good
speed through here gets a good drive onto the
Mountain Mile straight that follows, so it's one of those
critical places counting towards a really fast lap.

This photo was taken in 2009's Saturday practice, the
first un-timed session that begins the high excitement of
TT fortnight.

*"I believe that I have barely scratched the surface in
exploiting the potential of using remote cameras at the TT.
The only limits are the photographer's imagination and, of
course, rider safety. Long may the Isle of Man TT continue, the
world's oldest and greatest test of motorcyclist, machine and
shutter speed!"*

Dave Collister, Isle of Man 2010

www.photocycles.com

Ecstatic fans greet John McGuinness in Victory Lane after his superb 130mph Centenary ride in 2007.

We wish to thank John Lewis at Gomer Press, John McGuinness, Alan Perkin, David Purves and Mike Kelly at Mannin Collections. Dave Collister would also like to thank his wife Christine for her patience and his mother and father for ignoring his requests for a Scalextric set in 1978 and buying him his first camera instead.

Produced and Designed by Lily Publications Ltd

Printed and bound by Gomer Press Ltd., Wales © Lily Publications 2010